Autumn Scenes
Coloring Book

An Adult Coloring Book Featuring Beautiful
Autumn Scenes, Cute Animals and Relaxing
Fall Inspired Designs

COLORING BOOK
Cafe

an Imprint of **The Fruitful Mind Publishing LTD.**
www.coloringbookcafe.com

Have questions? Let us know.
support@coloringbookcafe.com

facebook.com/coloringbookcafe   @coloringbookcafe

This Book
Belongs To:

PUMPKINS for SaLe

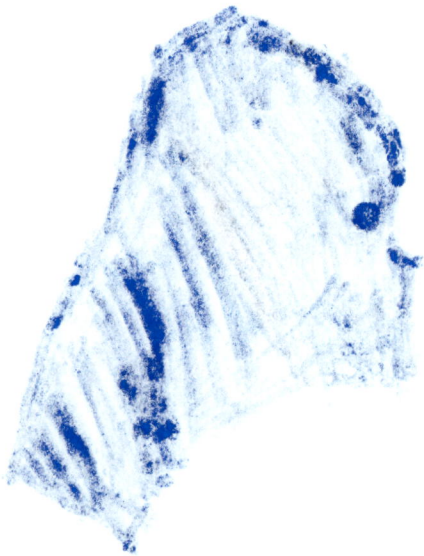